The Square Circle

by

Herbie Curtis

The Square Circle

©Herbert Curtis 1998

Cover illustration: Original artwork by Ryan Curtis

Proofing and typesetting: Ryan Curtis and Julia Knight

Inside photographs and illustrations: All images were kindly donated by Herbie's friends and family for use in this publication. Copyright remains with the respective owners.

Published by: Sculptural Images

Printed by: Ingram Spark

All rights reserved. No part of this publication may be reproduced, stored in a retrieval system or transmitted in any form or by any means, electronic mechanical, photocopying, recording or otherwise, without the prior permission of the publishers.

Dedication

I would like to dedicate this book to the memory of Mr Reginald Bosworth, Headmaster of Rudgeway C of E school, who spent three years trying to drum some education into my thick head and whom I'm sure would be amazed and delighted to find that fifty years on his hard work was not completely in vain.

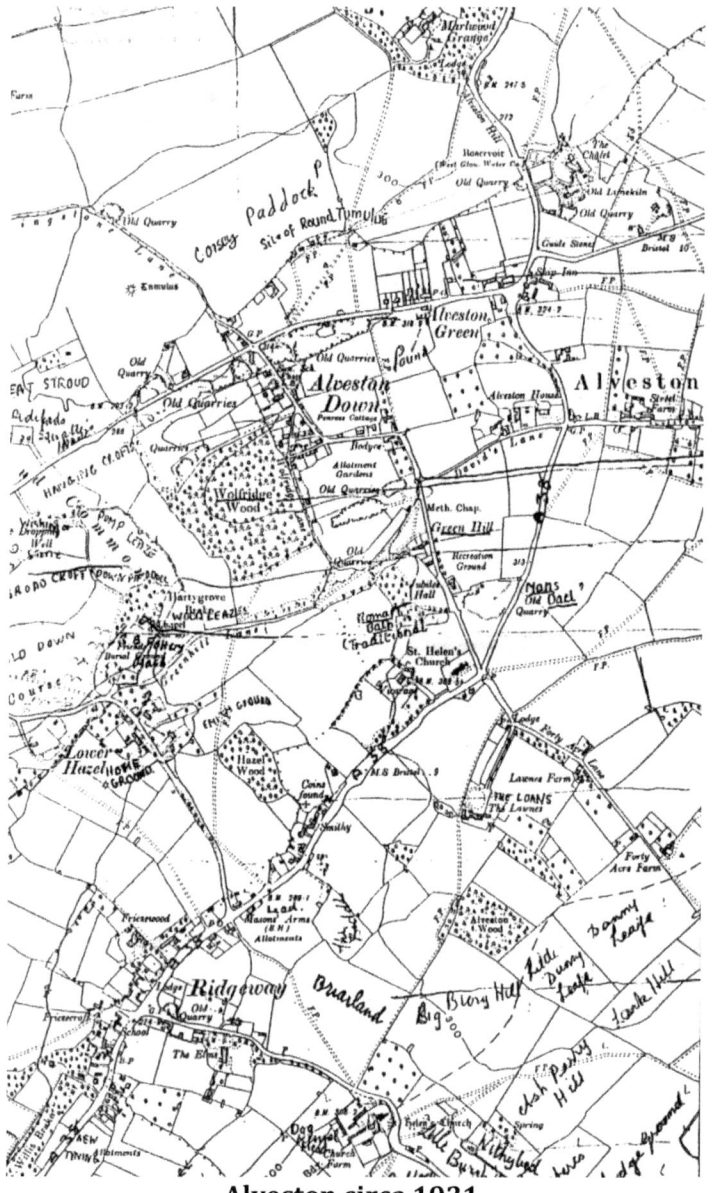

Alveston circa 1931

This map was supplied by a friend of the family and is not necessarily exact, for example Rudgeway is noted here as Ridgeway.

In this detailed view the arrow shows the location of

'The Square'

Foreword

For some time, I have been thinking of writing a book about the village of Alveston and its inhabitants, as I knew and remembered them in my youth. I didn't want it to be just another geography of a village but rather an insight into the way in which ordinary people of that time lived, and how they went about their everyday lives. Something on the lines of the late James Herriot author of All Creatures Great And Small, whom I greatly admired. I was finally pressurised into making a start after listening to a tape recording of the history of Alveston in the 1930's made by Mrs May Neate and kindly lent to us by her. Also under pressure from my wife and youngest son who convinced me that I owe it to future generations of Alvestonians and to history in general.

I decided to start at one end of the village and work from house to house describing the people who lived there and any little anecdotes or things of interest that I can remember about them. As you can imagine, things in Alveston have changed considerably over the last forty years and lots of things have happened like building estates, etc., to cause a complete transformation to the village and to the type of people who lived there. In view of this and so as not to be diverted by all these later happenings, I have decided to condense this book into the period between 1940 to 1955 which were my school days and the formative years of my youth and also the years of the Second World War and Post War years up until the time of my going into the Forces to serve my two years National Service. Some of the stories may be second hand but most are based on actual happenings. However, with the memory beginning to fail and things being shrouded in the mists of time I must beg for a bit of poetic licence from those who can remember better than myself. I'm quite sure my acquaintances of that time will remind me of lots of things which I have long since forgotten.

(Dear reader, please note that this memoir\tour is of The Square and folk as remembered by Herbie in the 1990's. People may have passed and the buildings changed in the intervening years.)

The Square Circle

The author's parents at the gate to their cottage

Herbie Curtis

Memories of Alveston

First of all I would like to tell you about myself and family and my qualifications for writing this book. As a person born and brought up in the locality, I shouldn't really need any qualifications. My name is Herbert Curtis, known to one and all as Herbie, I was born at the Inner Down at Old Down, one of a family of eight boys and three girls. My father was the late Jim Curtis who died in 1972. My mother was Dora Dyer who died in 1995 at the age of ninety two. My father at that time worked as a farm labourer for local farmer Mr Vowles, of Upper Hazel Farm.

We lived in a little cottage owned by the farmer consisting of two living rooms and two bedrooms, no water or electricity and a toilet at the bottom of the garden. We had to fetch our drinking water in milk churns from the pump on Old Down. As you can imagine conditions were so cramped in the house that my two eldest brothers had to sleep in a small tent in the orchard next door, summer and winter, whilst my eldest sister was put into service at a big house in Tockington to relieve the pressure on accommodation. We also at that time had my mother's father who was in his seventies living with us as well which didn't help matters much.

The farmer, who was on the local council, tried hard to get us council accommodation but it meant that they would have to knock two houses into one and they weren't prepared to do that.

I attended Old Down Infant School, which is now a private house next to the football pitch at the Plain at Old Down, under the care of governess Durnell. I can't remember a lot about those years but I do remember being given a Coronation Mug at the party at the park at Old Down by Mrs Turner, late of the mansion which is now the Kitchen Garden. I also remember my father holding me in his arms and pointing out to me an airship flying up the river Severn which I believe to be the R106, which was in 1936 or there about.

In 1939 when I was seven years old my father bought two adjoining cottages in the Square at Alveston which he made into one house to accommodate the tribe, and for the first time we all lived together. He never got around to removing one of the staircases and unto this day the house boasts two lots of stairs.

Inside 'The Square'- View of the second staircase, which was blocked off and used for storage.

I can vividly remember moving house and sitting with my other brothers on the pile of household effects on the back of my uncle's old Bedford lorry and watching the telegraph poles and trees flashing by and I thought that they were moving whilst we were stopped still. Eventually we settled into the Square and were accepted by the neighbours.

The younger element went to Rudgeway C of E School which was the forerunner to St Helens School today, under the guidance of headmaster Mr Reginald Bosworth and Mr F W Walmsley who was the vicar of St Helens at the time. The old school is still there but once again has been converted into a private house.

Anyway, this seems to be an appropriate time to start my reminiscences. As I stated earlier, I shall start where the Oldown Road enters Alveston, which is known as 'The Strode' or 'The Stroud'. Strictly speaking, this area at that time was not in the Parish of Alveston, but in the Parish of Olveston. However, it was so far distant that the people were to all intents and purposes classed as Alvestonians, and attended the local church, school and so on. It has since been absorbed into the parish by a recent boundary change.

The first cottage on the left was occupied by Mr Fred Cole who worked as a farm labourer for Mr Charles Hill at the Grove Alveston Street. I remember him telling my father that he had complained to Mr Hill about the amount of Income Tax he was paying.

Mr Hill evidently made him an offer that he would pay his tax for a whole year if Fred would pay his for one day. I don't think he took the offer up.

Fred had a son called Dick who because of his keen interest in anything mechanical especially motorbikes or cars earned himself the nickname of 'Sprocket'. He was a bit like Wesley in Last of the Summer Wine (1970's British sitcom). If you wanted anything mended or adapted Sprocket was the man to go to. He would disappear into his shed which was packed with lathes and tools of all descriptions and before long he had the job done. During the war he worked at the B.A.C Filton and he used to drive an old Ford Eight car to work rather than go on the bus like everyone else. Now at that time petrol was rationed and hard to come by so Sprocket adapted his car to run on paraffin. It started on petrol then when the engine was warm he switched it to paraffin. This worked quite well but you always knew when he had gone past because for sometime after you could see a cloud of blue smoke and smell paraffin in the air.

Another thing I remember Dick for; I went there one day with something for him to repair, a radio I think it was, and he invited me in and politely asked if I would like a cup of tea while I waited. I sat down at the kitchen table while he made the tea. He came back with two cups which he placed on the table, then he asked me to be careful not to spill tea on the tablecloth because he hadn't had time to read it yet, I believe it was the Bristol Evening Post. In the adjoining half of the cottage lived a relation of my mothers who I knew as uncle Ted but I didn't know much about him.

On the opposite side of the road surrounded by iron railings was the parish quarry. Next to that was my uncle Fred's limestone quarry in the depths of which he had built a bungalow in which he lived with his wife Gladys and my six cousins. This quarry was complete with limekiln and was being worked, certainly up until the 50's.

I think I should tell you how this limekiln worked because not many people know now. It was a square structure built out of stone with a firebrick lining. It was shaped like a funnel, with two bell shaped holes in the bottom on opposing sides, through which the burnt limestone was withdrawn. The method of firing it up went like this. First of all you filled the bottom with paper and straw. On top of this were placed the faggots of wood, then a layer of coke, followed by a layer of broken limestone, each piece no bigger than three inches in diameter. Then another layer of coke and another layer of stone. Then you lit it up and with a bit of luck away it went. This process of laying with coke and stone had to be done twice a day, seven days a week. Then the burnt stone was extracted from the bottom where it was barrowed into the shed where it was sold as lump lime or else it was put in a tank of water (slaked as we called it) where it was turned into lime putty to be used in mortar mixing or for lime washing.

We used to spend many a winter's night sitting on top of the kiln, roasting potatoes or apples. It was lovely and warm. During the war it was covered with a roof of galvanized iron so that German planes wouldn't see the glow. This was the last working quarry in the village, which had at one time boasted several. When my uncle died his sons took it over but they couldn't agree with one another so it closed down, was filled in and now a small estate has been built on it.

To go back to my uncle. He was a big strong man who worked hard. He was usually dressed in hobnailed boots, trousers that were ripped and torn at the knees and the back, with a torn shirt open at the neck to match. One day, he'd been having a row with his wife, which was not unusual. On his way out of the quarry he stopped the lorry and her what was for dinner, to which she replied "arsehole". Fred pulled away and shouted "Well only cook half 'cos I shan't be home."

He was also a great benefactor of the local boys football team and sponsored all of their kit and footballs. One morning he was stood on the touchline in his working clothes, which I have described, when they came around with the collection box. A very smart gentleman near Fred took out his wallet and put a pound note in. When they got to Fred he put his hand in his trouser pocket, pulled out a roll of notes, extracted a five pound note and calmly placed it in the box. Nobody upstaged my uncle.

On Sunday afternoons in the Summer Fred was in the habit of taking us kids in the back of his lorry down to Littleton-On-Severn to enjoy a bit of swimming in the river. When we finally arrived it was a relief to get in the water and wash the limedust out of our eyes. Now the road wasn't wide then and sometimes we would meet a car coming the other way. On these occasions there was a stand-off situation as to who was going to back up. Fred never gave in to anyone. He would switch his engine off and sit there reading the paper until the other person got fed up and moved. This was before the two nuclear power stations were built up the river. I think we would turn fluorescent green if we swum in it now!

On another occasion we went to the quarry to pick up our cousin to come and play football for the junior team. He was always late. We found him breaking up stone in the depths of the quarry. "I can't come until I finish this pile of stones" he said, "Or else our old man will murder I". There was only one thing to do. We all grabbed hammers and got stuck in. We got to the match just in time but tired out.

The next house on the left, where Strode Gardens stands now, was a fairly big stone built house called 'The Villa.' An old lady called Kitty Issacs lived here and she used to shuffle up the pavement with the aid of a walking stick, hanging on the wall and muttering to herself. She didn't like boys and woe betide you if you came in range of that stick. We thought she was a witch and kept well away from her.

Up in the field behind 'The Villa' lived Mr and Mrs Bunty Riddiford. Bunty was a local builder. He was also a keen bowls player and with Edgar Liddiatt and Jack Salter from the Post Office at Rudgeway. They kept the Bowling Green at Oldown in good condition throughout the war. His wife was a lovely woman who was involved in nearly every woman's organisation in Alveston, and she also had the added burden of being our Sunday School teacher at the Jubilee Hall.

Past 'The Villa' was a paddock which contained two bungalows. In one lived Harry Timbrell and family. Harry was a milkman and drove a three wheeled Reliant van. In the other lived Mr and Mrs Ralph Haddrell, and Ralph was a carpenter and cabinet maker.

Next door, at the top of a long garden, was a stone cottage in which lived Mr and Mrs Bill Neate and family. Bill used to ride a 125 James motorbike to work at Avonmouth and was a familiar sight phut-phutting up the Strode. He was also a familiar sight in the Cross Hands as it happens, because his mother was Landlady there. I've been told that he rode this motorbike with his wife on the pillion, visiting relations in Paignton, Devon on many occasions. Bearing in mind that there was no motorway in those day and it was over 100 miles this was no mean feat. He once told me that he used to break two raw eggs into a glass, and drink that every day of his life. At the front of this cottage was one of the community pumps where people used to get their water.

On the corner of Vattingstone Lane, opposite the Cross Hands pub, lived a retired farmer from Yorkshire called Mr Bates. Now Mr Bates was a portly gentleman and suffered from severe gout. On nice days his wife would push him up the road in a wickerwork bath chair. I remember one day in the early part of the war, his wife had pushed him up to the Post Office and was on her way home At that time the Germans were carrying out daytime raids on Filton Aircraft Works; on this particular day a dog fight had broken out in the skies above with planes wheeling and diving and machine gunning. Mr Bates became very alarmed by all this and thought he would be safer indoors, so entreated his wife to get a move on. Mrs Bates, being only a small woman, could not generate much speed so he leapt out of the chair and ran the rest of the way home, bandaged foot and all. We carried on playing football quite unconcerned.

In Vattingstone Lane in the adjoining part of Bill Neate's house lived Mr Alfie Williams and family. Alfie had a wooden leg and used to ride a bicycle with one pedal, how he managed this I don't know. In the cottage opposite lived an old man called Rocky Williams.

On the corner of Down Road and Vattingstone Lane where Haddrell Court now stands was the council depot and yard which was very busy in those days. Opposite was the Cross Hands public house which was run by Kate Neate. I used to think she was the image of Queen Victoria or at least of the pictures I had seen of her. Kate never left the pub and yet she knew everything which happened in the village in a very short time. One of the things I remember were the house martins that used to nest under the porch around the eaves and under the windows. There must have been about fifty nests and on warm summer nights we would sit on the bench outside the door eating our crisps and watch them swooping and circling so close you could almost touch them. In the fifties the pub was extensively renovated and the painters poked the nests out and the birds never returned.

The Cross Hands was the gathering place for all of us teenagers at that time, but we never made a nuisance of ourselves to the customers (who were mostly our parents anyway) or to 'Gran' as we called her. We were tolerated by May and Bill as necessary evils, I think. I remember going into the pub in my uniform whilst I was doing my National Service and Kate refused to serve me because I wasn't old enough. I think she thought I was in the Boy Scouts.

Going towards the church, on the left was another parish quarry where the Home Guard used to train. It contained a concrete bunker in which I supposed they used to store their spears, bows and arrows. In fact, they used to store bottles of petrol with paraffin wicks which they called Molotov Cocktails. We soon learned how to make these, and had great fun throwing them at one another up in Wolfridge Wood, which I will tell you about later. I think the late Mr Reg Allchurch was the commanding officer, ably assisted by Mr Bert Burgess. This quarry is now part of the local playing field.

Here I must tell a funny story concerning the Home Guard. They used to have at 'Friezewood', in Rudgeway, a dovecote in the grounds (it is still there) which overlooked the River Severn and was used as an observation post in case the Germans invaded by sea. It appears that one dark night whilst they were on guard, playing cards, one of their men, (a certain Art Moss, known as Sniper Moss because he was the only one with a shotgun) had been down to the Mason's Arms for a jug of cider. On the way back, he tripped over a tree root, and accidentally discharged his gun. He also dropped the jug of cider, which resulted in much cursing. Hearing this commotion, the men in the O.P. thought that the Germans had landed behind them, so they took flight and ran home to hide under the stairs. Whether there was any truth in this, I don't know. I do know that during our nightly chasing games, we very often ran into them, causing a lot of confusion.

We had made this device out of a cardboard tube and mirrors, which we called a 'Seebackroscope' so that we could peer around corners and also watch out for any assassins who might be creeping up on us from behind. If a stranger appeared in the village, he was immediately branded a German spy and we would follow him around to find out where he hid his secret wireless transmitter.

Now, before we proceed any further, I should like a little aside here because it is relevant to the next story. Myself, three of my brothers, my cousin, and a couple of friends - all between the ages of eight and thirteen - were known to the locals as the 'Curtis Commandos'. This was probably because of the silent and deadly raids which we carried out on people's apple orchards and plum trees, as well as other mischief we got up to. The relevance of this will soon become clear.

The Curtis Commandos

Behind the Methodist Chapel (which is now a private house) lived an old lady named Higgins, her daughter and son in law, who I think was called James. At the back of the house was an orchard containing trees of Cox's Orange Pippins, Beauty of Bath, Laxton Wonder, and other varieties of apples and pears. All of these were irresistible to the Curtis Commandos, and we used to raid this orchard on a regular basis. The son in law, however, was very possessive of the fruit. He vowed to stop us from stealing, and set about the task with a kind of dogged determination that was the hallmark of wartime Britain.

First of all he erected a three strand barbed wire fence around the perimeter. This was an utter waste of time - The Commandos were veterans of many a campaign on the local farms. He then tried reinforcing the defences with a six foot high chicken wire fence. We got hold of a pair of wire snips, and cut holes in it. Next he resorted to modern technology, and put an electric fence around the wire. This stumped us for a while, until we discovered that by leaning a steel bar on the fence, we could short it out into the ground and render it harmless. (bear in mind that our limited education certainly didn't cover electronics, but where there's a will...)

The son in law then decided it was time to escalate the arms race and got himself a dog, which he allowed to roam free in the orchard. Where he acquired this so called dog, I have no idea. Appearing to be a cross between an alligator, a Tasmanian devil, and a mincing machine, it should have been in a Greek Epic, not a rural orchard! After a couple of encounters with this hound from Hell, the

Commandos were forced to admit defeat and go in search of easier pickings.

Across the road from the chapel was a little stone walled enclosure containing the graves of members of the Higgins and Haddrell family. Next door to the chapel was English's grocery store and bakery. The smell of freshly baked bread issuing from the bake house every morning was something I will never forget. I think we would have killed anyone to get our hands on one of Mr English's delicious lardy cakes. We seldom could afford to buy one, not even when we all pooled our pennies together. I used to work for Mrs English on Saturday mornings doing odd jobs looking after the garden, cleaning the chicken houses out, or if it was raining, chopping firewood or whitewashing the storerooms, all for the princely sum of two shillings for four hours.

At that time there was no such thing as display cabinets in the shops. All sweets and chocolates etc. were displayed on the counter, so we used to go into the shop in a group and while one distracted the server's attention, the others were stealing things off of the counter. I believe this practice is still done by the modern youth. Now Jack English was quite aware of this game and one day he exchanged all the chocolate for laxative chocolate. Sure enough we weren't long in stealing it, and then spent the next twelve hours living in the toilet. The next time I went into the shop, Jack politely enquired whether I had gotten over my severe attack of gastro-enteritis and was there any truth in the rumour that I had had to 'go to ditch' as he put it four times during the football match. That put paid to the shoplifting for a bit.

Mrs English was also a character in her own right. I remember that one of her favourite jokes went like this: The salmon and the sole were swimming in the sea when they accidentally bumped into one another, the sole said 'Ah! Salmon', the salmon replied 'Ah! Sole'. Then she would go off into the back of the shop chuckling to herself.

Their nephews, Frank and Brian, also worked in the bakehouse and on the delivery rounds. Frank sadly died recently but Brian still lives opposite in a bungalow which he built on the site of the old garden and chicken run. Unfortunately this shop and bakery couldn't cope with progress and is now closed down and converted into a private house. Next door to the shop lived Mr and Mrs Raymond Hadrell. I remember the post box that used to be in the garden wall of this house.

Further on up the alley was a pair of semi detached stone cottages. In the first lived Mr Joss Vizard and family. He was a local bricklayer. In the other one lived another relation of my mother called Oliver Wedgebury and wife. Now he wore a surgical boot with a very thick sole on one foot. One day we asked him why he wore this, he told us that when he was a young man he went to Canada and joined the mounted police. He was trailing some criminals in the Northern Territories when they ambushed and shot him and left him for dead in the snow. He wasn't discovered for some time afterwards as a result of which he suffered severe frostbite and had to have his toes and two of his fingers amputated. When we expressed disbelief at this he opened his shirt and showed us two blue puncture marks in his chest which he claimed were bullet holes. I never discovered if this story was true but I believed it anyway.

In the row of cottages across the road from the alley lived Mr and Mrs Algie Hobbs and daughters. Mr Hobbs was our hairdresser - Short back and sides variety. Next-door was Fred and Mrs Hurcombe and sister-in-law Violet Poseland. Fred was a special constable in the War years. In the end house lived Mr and Mrs Francis Clutterbuck and daughters who are still living in the village at the time of writing.

In the big house opposite, called 'Quarry House', lived two lovely old ladies called Masters, always known as Miss Alice and Miss Carrie. They were very kind to us and often gave us sixpence to buy sweets, they were always good for half crown at Christmas time when we went there carol singing. My younger brother used to work there on Saturday mornings and during the school holidays.

They had a brother called Arthur who owned a big clothing store in Cardiff and every now and again they would measure my brother up and buy him a new suit and shoes. As we were all about the same size we took it in turn to wear these suits if we had to go anywhere special. Also at that time a man by the name of Mr Milton who I think also came from Cardiff, used to come around every fortnight or so selling clothing and my mother used to buy our suits off of him and pay so much when she could afford it.

Behind 'Quarry House', up on the bank, were the Locks. He was a cobbler and shoe repairer. Across the road at the bottom of the hill lived Charlie English and family, brother of Jack at the shop, and a very cheerful fellow always humming. He used to call me Herbert the Sherbert or Herbot the Turbot.

View across the quarry to Methodist Chapel and English's shop

We now take the right hand fork that leads up the hill to The Square, which was the stronghold of the Curtis commandos. At the bottom of this hill on the right was a little stone cottage in the garden of which stood a lovely old walnut tree which overhung the road. Every Autumn without fail, it produced a huge crop of walnuts which eventually ripened and fell into the road and was eagerly snapped up by us eager boys, providing we got there before the crows. This cottage was owned by the Chambers family in The Square.

At the top of the hill facing you was a pair of cottages in the shape of an L. In the end one lived Mr

Walter Clark, known to us as Gramfee, and his dog Tim. He worked in English's shop as a baker and also cut hair at weekends. In the cottage facing towards the Square lived Charlie and Minnie Biddle, very good neighbours of our family. Many were the times that Charlie intervened in family disputes and saved one or other of us from getting a good hiding, while Min would do anything to help anybody.

Past there and set back in was another cottage in which lived an old lady called Laura Stockton. She kept very much to herself and we didn't know much about her. Next to that was Laurel Cottage where lived Mr Edgar Liddiat and wife. He owned the local charabanc which took us on our annual Sunday School trips to Weston-Super-Mare. He was also a keen bowls player and played in one of the local brass bands – Tytherington, I think.

In the middle of The Square stood the village pump where we all used to get our drinking water; it used to boast a stone trough in front, but this has gone now although the pump remains.

Behind the village pump was a pair of cottages in which lived Harold and Charlie Clark and families; they were local builders and sons of Gramfee Clark whom I just mentioned. They had just returned from war service and had brought their families up there.

At the side of these cottages was an alleyway which led to the back of The Square and was much used by us as a short cut to the allotments and our friends at the rear. There's been a lot of dispute regarding right of way recently but this alley was used regularly by us up till the seventies and eighties.

Proceeding down Wolfridge Lane, in the cottage on the right lived Wedger and Doris Collins and family. Wedger was also a keen bandsman and played a huge bassoon, I think it was. He used to sit out in the middle of Wolfridge Wood and practice on this instrument, out of the way of his wife. Opposite lived, Mr and Mrs Jack Mills. I have still got various planes and woodworking tools which Jack gave me when he retired.

Just below the Mills was a stone cottage running parallel with Wolfridge Lane. In this lived Mr Arthur Stevens and family, this cottage was demolished in the late fifties or early sixties. Halfway down the lane lived Mr and Mrs 'Whale' Collins and sons Frank and Harry. He used to be a part time Postman and also worked on the local rubbish tip.

I remember coming home from school sometime late in the war to find that an aeroplane had crashed in their front garden, a Mustang I think it was, one wing was along the front of the cottage blocking the front door and it was burning fiercely. Mrs Collins was upstairs making the beds at the time and she never heard a thing until the fire engines arrived. One of the boys said "Crikey, look what old Whale has brought home from the tip now!" The pilot of this aircraft was killed while attempting to bail out and was lying in the garden beside his half opened parachute. Whilst the men were engaged in putting out the fire, we boys stole the parachute and for ages after the local women were wearing underskirts made from this nylon, while the cords made excellent strings for our bows.

Now Harry Collins used to keep goats and he built a new house to accommodate some new arrivals; he put two doors in this house, a big one and a little one, and when asked why he needed two doors he explained that the big door was for the big goats and the little door was for the little goats, not realising that they could all use the big one!

At the bottom of the lane lived Mr Harry Collins, local postman and brother of Whale, and his wife who was known to us as Sally Duck, again I haven't a clue why.

Returning back up the lane and turning right behind the Mills lived an old chap called Joe Summers, he was a bit of a recluse. Next to that lived Mr and Mrs

Bob Taylor. Next door was a big house which had lots of people coming and going, mostly evacuees from the south of England; we never got to know these very well.

Opposite was a house and shop of Mr Stanley Chambers and family, he was another local shoe repairer and cobbler and as you can imagine did a good trade with all us boys. We used to hand our shoes down as we grew out of them and I can remember going to school with one football boot on one foot and a plimsoll on the other, nobody laughed or took the mickey because they were mostly all in the same boat.

On the corner in the big red house named 'Wolfridge Villa' lived Mr Tom Collins senior, again a musician and devout church goer, chief bell ringer and choir master; he had a very deep baritone voice which was unmistakable during church services. In the other half of 'Wolfridge Villa' lived an old man called Mr Moore, retired carpenter and wheelwright; he had a great big greyhound which used to jump up on the wall and frighten us kids to death.

Opposite this, where a row of new houses now stand, was a little cottage in which lived Acker and Connie Curtis, no relation to us, I had heard tell that

Acker was a very good cricketer and a bowler of county standard in his younger days.

Further along towards The Square up along a garden path and opposite our house lived Mr and Mrs Walt Biddle and their daughter Amy. He was a retired coach painter and sign writer. Mrs Biddle was known to us all as Gran and she and Amy were involved with the church, women's Institute, Red Cross, Sunday School, you name it they were part of it. Nearly everything that happened in the village revolved around the local ladies groups. Our bedroom window overlooked Gran's garden and on washing days she would hang out these immense silk bloomers on the line to dry; we used to get in our bedroom window with an air rifle and take pot shots at them but we never managed to put a hole in them.

Our neighbours had a lot to put up with I can tell you. In the summer mother used to put us to bed early if she could get us in, so we used to lie in bed singing until it got dark. One day Gran said to her "Your Herbert's got a voice like a little thrush. I'm going to see the Vicar and see if I can get him in the choir." She had been in her garden and had heard us singing.

White cottage in The Square

In the little cottage next door to us and opposite Gran's front gate lived her son Victor and his wife Madge; they brought up six children in that one up, one down house. My elder brother bought it in the early fifties when they left, for ninety pounds, which was his gratuities from the R.A.F.

Retracing our steps and turning left, on the corner stood a cottage in which Bob Boulton and family lived. Again he was a coach builder and wheelwright, and here was kept the local village bier, which was used to transport coffins to the church.

Halfway down the hill on the left lived Oliver Eacott. Now Ollie was a bit of a cider man, and I well remember watching him going up to the Cross Hands at 12 o'clock on Sunday closely followed by his black cat, tail in the air. That cat would wait outside until Ollie came staggering out at closing time then follow him back home again. Oliver's son Rodney once told me that for years after Ollie died he would come across flagons of cider which his dad had buried in the garden and forgotten where he'd put them. When we went there carol singing we had a special carol for him. It went "The first tree in the greenwood, it was the holly" and we would put great emphasis on 'holleee'. The result was that Ollie would rush out with his belt and chase us up the road.

Back up the hill and bearing left along Greenhill Road, on the left from the top of the hill there were fields as far as The Ship Hotel. It is now a huge housing estate. Following the garden wall around, you came to a pair of cottages. In the first lived Mrs Saxton and her son and daughter. Her husband was a prisoner of war, having been taken by the Japanese when Singapore fell. For a long time nobody knew whether he was alive or dead. Happily, at the end of the war he arrived back home, to a rapturous welcome.

While we are on this subject let me tell you that my brother was in the RAF and my sister was a Sergeant cook in the WAAF. She was awarded a Mention in Despatches ribbon with oak leaves, whilst my cousin, who was in the Royal Navy, was awarded the B.E.M. We were understandably very proud of this and were very glad to see them all back home again.

In the second cottage of the pair, 'Lily Cottage', lived my uncle Tom and wife and three cousins. Tom was the local woodcutter and with my dad and 'Bobeye' Vizard, whom I shall deal with later, they were part time poachers as well. Tom's son, daughter and grandson still live there now.

Further along on the left was another pair of cottages. In the first lived Mr Sid Haines and wife, and children. Mrs Haines was still living there at the time of writing, aged 93 years.

Next door lived Mr Gilbert Collins, wife Joan and family. Joan was another stalwart of the village, involved in everything and always helping other people, in fact she was knocked down and killed whilst out selling poppies one dark night. Gilbert, like all the Collins's was a keen musician and bell ringer at St Helens church. During the war it was not permitted to ring a full peal of bells, as this was kept as a warning of invasion by the Germans, so on Sunday mornings Gilbert used to play hymns using a single bell, of course, he had eight bells to choose from, but I never found out how he did it. I can still remember as a child lying on the grass in the Jubilee Hall field and listening to him playing Abide with Me, All Creatures Great and Small and other popular hymn. He was also a very keen sportsman and could always be found leaning on the wall up by The Ship Hotel watching Thornbury Cricket Club play someone or other.

On the right of the road opposite these cottages was an allotment, my father had two pieces of garden here and I spent many a miserable time digging and weeding when I would much rather have been playing football or cricket.

A West Country allotment

Continuing on the left stood a house on its own called 'Penrose'. This was owned by Mr Jammy James and family. Now Jammy was an Australian sea captain (retired), he also had a piece of allotment next to ours. Now from the road level to the allotments was a drop of some 10ft or so and to save himself walking up to the gate to the allotments and back, Jammy installed an iron ladder which he used to climb down.

Bearing in mind that few people in Alveston had a W.C or water, Mr James every so often would take his full toilet bucket to his allotment and dig a hole and bury it. Now one day I was digging for victory when he came along the road with his bucket, balanced on the wall and climbed on to his ladder, I don't know whether his foot slipped or what, but the result was that the bucket over balanced and went all down him, Well, I can tell you the air was blue and I learnt some swear words that day that even I didn't know existed.

Jammy was a good storyteller and whilst we were working on our respective lots, he would tell me about his life in Australia as a boy and how he came to join the merchant navy and eventually rise to the rank of captain. The then prime minister of Australia, Mr Robert Menzies, was a personal friend of his and he would show me letters which they had exchanged at that time.

Past 'Penrose', on the corner where the shops now stand, was a farm house in which lived Mr and Mrs Warren. In front of this, behind the garden wall and looking up Greenhill Road towards the church, was a machine gun post with apertures in the wall to fire through. Also I remember a big tree trunk on a cart wheel which the Home Guard used to trundle across the road to block it.

Opposite on this corner was 'The Bodyce' in which lived Mr and Mrs Percy Savery, an agriculture engineer. They had a lovely orchard containing a big walnut tree and lots of Morgan Sweet apples, another regular target for the Commandos. This orchard is now built on, but I lived in a caravan there for 2 years when I first married. I think there were six caravans and a wooden bungalow in which lived Mr and Mrs Gould. Opposite the corner was yet another village pump.

Along the road you could turn left up Davids Lane. There were no houses until you came to Bob Champion's farm, just a narrow lane with corn fields on each side. I can remember that one day they were cutting corn in the field behind the Riding School where Davids Close now is, the binder used to go around in ever decreasing circles until there was only a small patch left in the middle. Eventually all the rabbits and things had to flee for their lives, to be met with shotguns or stones from us boys. Now Chippy had a labourer called Sid Clutterbuck working for him and Sid was getting on a bit, and his eyesight wasn't all that good, This day he was in charge of the shotgun, he was also in charge of the dog Tiger, which was a collie sheepdog. Anyway, a fox ran out of the corn straight towards Sid. We were all shouting at him to shoot it, but he thought it was the dog and was calling "Tiger, Tiger get back", needless to say Reynard made his escape.

Opposite, where the road now goes to Wolfridge Ride, was the local council quarry which was still in operation at that time. They would quarry the stone and then load it by hand onto small skips which ran up on rails pulled by a small winch. Then it went into hoppers and was eventually coated with tarmac and taken by lorry to repair the roads. This quarry closed down in the 50's, was filled in, and is now another estate. Beyond the quarry there were just open fields and woodland down to Lower Hazel.

On the right behind a line of iron railings was Greenhill, in the bottom corner of which was the little Methodist Chapel presided over by Mr James Olive of

Lower Hazel Farm, a true Christian if ever there was one. I think he was the last person to be buried in the old church at Rudgeway. They were unable to deconsecrate the church until he died because his family had bought a communal grave way back.

One of the old churches of Alveston

Along the top of Greenhill was a row of cottages (still there) in which lived Mr and Mrs Pop Collins and their family. Next door were Fred and Ivy Grove. Fred was a motorbike fanatic and his bikes were the envy of us teenagers.

Next to them in the end cottage lived and old ex-carpenter called 'German' Nicholls, who walked with a very funny gait, as one person described as 'sitting back in his braces". This poor chap was the subject of much mickey taking by us yobbos which, I can realise now, must have hurt.

Opposite the Jubilee Hall field lived Mr and Mrs Fred Williams and daughter Margaret. Fred was verger and head cook and bottle washer at St Helens Church. Margaret still lives there at time of writing. Where the road now goes into Underwood Close was a pair of semi detached stone built cottages (now demolished) in which lived Mr Bill Smith. Bill was the Alveston Down Sports Goalkeeper at that time and well lived up to his nickname of Tiger. His wife Becky still lives just up the road.

The Jubilee Hall

Next door was his mother Mrs Bowyer, who will never be forgotten by us footballers. This old lady for years used to boil the water for us to bath in after the match. She would carry this over to the Jubilee Hall in buckets, which took her most of the afternoon. I don't know if she ever got paid for this, but I can't see anyone doing that today.

All the way along the road opposite the Hall were council houses. Starting from the church end lived the Gales, Mr and Mrs Jack Withers, then Graham Vizard. I remember here that we were out in the road by the Hall playing and shouting as kids do, when Mrs Vizard came out and chased us off saying that we should be ashamed of ourselves for making such a din whilst her husband was indoors dangerously ill and dying. Graham only recently died at the grand old age of 102, whilst she has been dead for years.

Next door lived my mother's brother Tom 'Tanty' Dyer and Auntie Min. Tom used to work for Mr Bush of 'Alveston House'. One day, they were felling a huge tree in the grounds, while Mr Bush stood watching. Tanty shouted to him "Stand clear, Mr Bush Sir, the trees about to leave its destination!"

During the annual occasion of Alveston flower and horticultural show, which was usually held in August at the Jubilee Hall ground, a big Marquee was erected for the produce and competitors. People who were unable to attend on the day would leave their entries in the marquee over night. To prevent any theft or jiggery pokery, Uncle Tom would sit in a chair with a shotgun all night, keeping guard. There was also a funfair held at the same time, but this was discontinued because of the mess the vehicles made of the football pitch.

Next to my uncle Tom Dyer's house lived Mr and Mrs Sage and son John, who earned the nickname of 'Tyke' given to him by his father, known to us even now as Tykie. Next door was Mr and Mrs Mackie Vizard and wife and family. Then the Savery's who will be remembered forever. Mr Savery left Mrs Savery to bring up the family on her own from an early age, helped by her daughter Norma and son Dennis. She overcame a lot of hard times and kept the family together, at the same time earning the respect of all her neighbours. It was sad to see the end of an era with the death of Norma recently.

In the next house is my uncle Harry and his wife, who recently celebrated her 100th birthday. Uncle Harry used to love his flowers and always wore one in his buttonhole which earned him the nickname of Swank or Springer. I remember meeting him in the Cross Hands bar, and like a dutiful nephew I asked him if he would like a half pint of beer, to which he replied "Half a soul was never saved my boy. I'll have a pint if you don't mind". What a joker! His son Lesley is a proper chip off the old block, Springer will never be dead for me as long as Les is alive.

Further down lived Mr and Mrs Bill Wesley and family. Bill was a staunch supporter of Alveston Junior boys team, and with my uncle Fred did much to promote junior football in Alveston. Next door lived Mr and Mrs Rodney Webb and daughters.

Rodney did very much to help mould my young life as I was then a would-be painter and decorator and learned the trade under him. I can honestly say that I never ever saw him in a miserable mood, he was always laughing and whistling and was a familiar sight riding up the road on his old bike, with a cheery wave and "Hello" to everyone he met. Yes, I missed old Rod a lot when he died. I well remember that Rodney had a little verse which he would write on the wall of a room he was wall papering, and it went like this:-

Rodney Webb is my name,

England is my nation,

Alveston is my dwelling place

and Christ is my salvation.

When I'm dead and buried

and my bones have all gone rotten

strip off this paper and you will see

that I AM NOT FORGOTTEN.

To which he added the date. For years after when I was decorating I would come across this verse and he was right, he was not forgotten. I wish more people could be like him - utterly content with his life.

Rodney was also the local bookies runner and collected all the local money, especially on Derby or Grand National. He would take this money home in a bag and on weekends it was my job to go to his house, collect the bag and take it on my bicycle to the bookie at nearby Thornbury. Then I would pick up any returns the next day and take the bag back. For this I received the princely sum of 2/6. One day, I had been to his house to pick up the bag which I put inside my shirt. As I came up the path from his house I was startled when the local policeman, PC Keane, suddenly sprang out of the bushes and grabbed me by the shoulder. "Got you now young Curtis, haven't I."

Of course at that time it was illegal to bet with an unregistered bookie and I was terrified.

"Give me that bag you've got inside your shirt", he said. I handed it over and he produced a betting slip and some money from his uniform pocket and put it in the bag. He explained he couldn't go down Rodney's with it because he was in uniform and a very shaken and relieved me went on my way.

Moving on up the road past the church field where the school now stands, we come to St. Helens church, and here I must decide which way to go. Forgetting the right turn to Rudgeway for the moment, we go straight across the road and up Forty Acres Lane. No houses on the right where the bungalows now stand, but a public footpath to the old church at Rudgeway. On the bend was the lodge to 'The Lawns', in which lived the Reynolds family. Beryl Reynolds and her brother Claude had lived in the big house originally, but after the war it was sold, and they moved into the lodge. During the war she was a captain in the Wrens, and could she tell some stories!

On up the lane, in the first farm lived Cyril and Graham Wonnacott and family. Again, firm chapel people, and friends of Jimmy Olive. They were known to us as the 'One-o-Clocks'.

Further up the lane was Mr Leslie Varney and family at 'Briar Mead'. Mr Varney was a market gardener and fruitier, and his son John has only recently ceased trading. He used to deliver into Bristol and around the local pubs. Whenever he parked his lorry to deliver to the Cross Hands or Mason's Arms, we used to steal oranges and bananas, etc. off the back. Les, of course, knew this, and used to put all the rotten fruit where it was easy to get at, so foiling us on many occasions. At the very top of the lane was another farm, in which lived the Champion family.

Coming back down the lane and turning right-handed onto the A38, we find on our left, where the playing field is now, a piece of rough quarry land known as 'The Tumps'. This is where the soldiers used to practise with their AA guns and searchlights. At one time they had a battery of 3.7 ack ack guns stationed there, and when they opened fire at night our poor old house used to shake.

Next we come to a row of houses on the same side. In the first was Addie Riddiford. In the bungalow next door lived Mr and Mrs 'Clem' Clements. Clem used to play the piano at the Cross Hands on Saturday nights for the weekly sing-along. I can't remember who lived in the next house (I think it was the Brain family), but the house after that had a little shop in the front room which sold cigarettes, papers, hair cream, etc. It was run by one 'Bunter' Sainsbury. We boys used to club together and buy five Woodbines off of him every now and again.

Next to him was Mr was Mrs Charlie Denning. In the front of the house was a lovely row of bright blue Hydrangea bushes, and Mrs. Denning always invited people to come and see her 'Hydraniums', much to our amusement. Next to the Dennings, was a bungalow occupied by Mr and Mrs Potter, and in the end house lived Mr Bill Ball, who I believe was the local council steamroller driver.

In one of these houses, someone had a pet parrot which they used to keep in a cage at the back, which adjoined the football pitch. This parrot had learned how to imitate the sound of the referee's whistle. Many a time a player had got clean through and then stopped for the whistle thinking he was offside, only to discover it was this pesky parrot.

Just past here on the left was The Riding School, a long wooden building with big skylights. It was taken over by the army during the war, as was the Jubilee Hall ground, and was occupied by the Maritime Regiment of the Royal Artillery. A lot of the soldiers married local girls and made their homes in the village.

One thing I remember about that period was that we children would go to the Jubilee Hall field around Christmas time, where we would be invited into one of the Nissen huts full of soldiers. We then sang carols, accompanied by various musical instruments, such as mouth organs, tin whistles, bells, and of course the soldiers, who thoroughly enjoyed the reminder of home. Afterwards they had a collection for us, but the best part of all was when they toasted bread on the iron tortoise stove, which stood in the middle of the hut, and spread it with baked beans, which of course we couldn't get at home. Oh! What luxury. We did a different hut every other night. Among these troops were quite a few professional footballers, who had nothing better to do than teach us their skills. No wonder Alveston Down Sports had such a good team in the fifties.

Halfway down Davids lane was Mr Bertie Champion's farm, which is still there. He was known by one and all as 'Chippy Champion' and I can vividly remember him delivering milk to us in the Square with his milk cart pulled by 'Maggie', a lively mare who always seemed to be ready to take off into the distance, so that he was constantly saying "Whoa

Maggie." You would go out with your jug and he would fill it with a measure from milk churns which he carried in the cart. He used to call me 'Bust Waistcoat' because I was a bit chubby. The family later moved up the road to The Street, where son Robert still farms.

Behind the farm (which is now called The Paddocks) was a lovely old half-timbered house called 'Oak House', occupied by local woodwork teacher Dickie Boreham. He taught us woodwork at Thornbury Council School every Monday morning, but to little avail, because I can't saw straight to this day. He was a very nice man though. Eventually he moved to Devon, and the house was knocked down to make way for a new building.

At the top of Davids lane was 'Alveston House', which at that time was a private building owned by people called Mellor. It was actually an old people's retirement home. Now it is the Alveston House Hotel. Directly opposite on the other side of David's Lane was a little green on which stood a bench seat, this was surrounded by tall elm trees. We used to sit on this seat on summer nights and wave to all the coaches coming back from Weston-Super-Mare on their way back to the Midlands. In the early fifties one of these elm trees blew down during a gale onto a passing car killing the occupants. They were then cut down and the road widened.

Across the A38 was The Street, I could never understand why it was called that when it was nowhere near the centre of Alveston. On the left was 'Champions Farm', further on up was a house owned by an eccentric lady named Miss Osborne. She was something to do with the R.S.P.C.A and had a passion for collecting lost or abandoned animals and birds, if you had a cat or rabbit you didn't want she was the person to go to and tell her that you'd found it.

Now she had a man working for her who did the garden and other odd jobs, he was known as 'Nailer' Weekes and was quite a joker. I remember him asking me if I had ever seen a water otter, as Miss Osborne had one round the back of the house in the shed. He took me around there and opened the shed door, he showed me this black kettle which he said was the biggest water hotter he'd ever seen, then he nearly collapsed laughing at the look on my face. He caught me again later with the same thing, only this time it was Miss Osborne's sawing horse. Yes, quite a joker was old Nailer!

Past there was a row of cottages, in the first one, called 'Walnut Tree Cottage', lived Nailer and his wife. The rest were occupied by gardeners, and employees of the Hill Estate. Then there was the large house known as 'The Grange', this was occupied by people called Holman at that time but I think was owned by the Hill Estate.

Right at the top of the street was 'The Grove', a beautiful house owned by Bristol ship builder Charles Hill. He employed most of the people who lived in the street either as farm labourers, gardeners, valets etc. A very good place for carol singing, half a crown was commonplace here.

Opposite was the big old farm called Alveston House Farm owned by 'Scrump' Chambers as we called him. He also delivered milk locally and especially to St Helens school. This came in little half pint bottles which had cardboard tops with a hole in the middle which you pressed to get the straw in. I can see those bottles now with the caption on 'A O Chambers, Channel Island Milk, accredited Guernsey Herd'. He was very proud of his cows and with good reason, it was nearly half cream. When he and his wife died, his son Henry and daughter Sarah had a new house built in the paddock called 'The Shepherds', in which they still live.

Coming back down the street on the corner was Mr 'Marm' Hadrell's farm. His wife Maggie was a parish and county councillor for a great many years in the fifties and sixties. Marm always did his farmwork with horses, but in the war he came up to date and purchased an old iron wheeled Fordson tractor, which his farm labourer used to drive. One day Johnny was ploughing a field whilst Marm was stood by watching. I think that Johnny was looking behind at the furrows when the tractor hit a bump and lurched sideways, throwing the unprepared Johnny out of the side. Luckily he fell clear, but the tractor went on alone, with poor old Marm, who didn't understand machinery, running beside and belabouring it with his stick and shouting "Whoa, you bugger, whoa!". Eventually it ran into the ditch where it stalled, much to Marm's relief. Johnny couldn't get up to help where he was laughing so much.

On the left again were cottages owned by the Hills. In the first lived Doug Niblett and family. Next were the family of Bishops. In between these was a carpenters shed owned by Charlie Jobbins who made farm carts. Then came Mr and Mrs Fred Dodd and family. Mr Dodd was Mr Hill's head gardener. I was told by Rodney Webb that before the thirties there was a big white house on the corner that used to be the local Post Office before it was demolished to make way for road widening.

Back across the A38 and right towards Thornbury. The two bungalows behind the hotel were built in the fifties. Then came a row of semi's, in the first one lived Mr and Mrs Simms who's son Cecil was a great pal of mine. In the middle one lived Stan Dyer and family. Now Stan was yet another of our hairdressers, short back and sides type. He was a chain smoker, and I don't think I ever saw him without his dog end dangling from his mouth. Then came another two semi's, the end one was a clothes shop run by a Mrs Tarbuck, this later became Pugsleys mini supermarket, where you could get almost anything.

On the opposite side of the road was Hawkins garage; at that time just a couple of pumps and a repair shed. Mr and Mrs Hawkins were killed in a car crash near Westonbirt and the garage was then run by Derek and Pat, again very good friends of ours. Next to that was Thornbury Cricket pitch where we spent many hours watching our heroes, especially visiting touring teams, I never saw the legendary W G Grace, but I did see his nephew (I think) Dr E M Grace, on many occasions.

Opposite the cricket ground was a big house owned by Dudley Cullimore who had a drapers shop in Thornbury High Street. Next to that was another big house in which lived Mr and Mrs Bill Essex. Mr Essex was a chauffeur to Mrs Commaline who lived in Orchard House around the corner. Next to that was a big orchard owned by Mr Chippy Champion. One night we were raiding this orchard and we had left our bicycles on the side of the road. Now Chippy was on his way to The Ship for his nightly tipple and caught us red handed! He confiscated our bikes and wouldn't let us have them back until we apologised, which we finally had to do. As Chippy remarked " 'pologising, doan bring me apples back do it?" He was one of the few people who ever caught us. He gave us a good dressing down and let us go.

In the corner of this orchard, where the bus shelter now is, there were some old barns, in front of which was a big pull-in. In here was a tin shed which was 'Annie's' cafe. This was run by a woman called Annie Silvey. It was the haunt of all the local lorry drivers, and also most of the village kids. Now Annie used to make the most wonderful meat pies soaked in gravy, I never tasted anything like them before in my life. So we used to run errands and help her around the place, just to get one of these pies. But sometimes all we got was the delicious smell because, of course, we could never afford to buy one. At that time you used to get 2p back on an empty lemonade bottle and Annie kept her empties around the back of the shed. You can guess what happened, we used to nick a couple and go round the front, collect the money and Bingo! One lovely pie. She never twigged on this as far as I know. Unfortunately, poor Annie was knocked down and killed by an American army coach whilst she was crossing the A38.

In the house on the corner I think people came and went and I never really got to know them. Then there was the big green known as The Ship Green, where the Bristol to Thornbury bus stopped. Now why I mention this is because the Hawkins' (from the garage back up the road) had a black dog with a curled up tail called Rip (not his tail, the dog I mean). Now Rip would wait on the stop till the bus came, then he would hop on and get under the stairs. No conductor was ever brave enough to try to chuck him off. He would go into Thornbury, then when he had completed his business he would catch the bus back up again, he did this for years.

Opposite the green was The Ship Hotel, now the Post House Motel. In those days the Berkeley hunt met there every Boxing Day, attracting hundreds of people both local and from Bristol. Past The Ship on the right was Old Gloucester Road. In one of the houses up here lived Dr E.M Grace, nephew of the great W.G. Grace I believe. Past that turning was the house of Dr Henderson, well known local GP and great benefactor to Thornbury hospital, where you can find a ward named after him. Below that was 'The Chalet', a big house set back in and owned by the Hignell family.

The Ship Hotel

Opposite there was a market garden behind a big wall. This was owned and worked by people called Ely. Outside of this house on the bank at the side of the road, there grew a plant with big broad leaves and people used to come and pick the leaves or roots, I understand to make medicine. There is still a big patch further on down the hill at this time.

Back up the hill to The Ship Green and right towards Oldown. On the corner lived Mr Rugg who had the chemists shop in Thornbury. The other house was lived in by various workers from The Ship. Next door in the long bungalow lived an American couple called Colston, very nice people.

Further down was 'Orchard House', owned by an eccentric lady called Mrs Commalline. She is still remembered for owning a lovely old Buick car, which was always chauffeur driven and immaculate - I wish I owned it now! We used to do a lot of maintenance work here, she had a little Sealyham dog called Lovell, which had boundless energy and his favourite game was to bring you a ball which you had to throw, no matter how far or how you hid it, he always found it and brought it back and he would keep this up all day. At the end of the day I was on my knees. Mrs C always called me Albert and I can still hear her voice saying "Go and get the ball for Albert, Lovell dahling".

From The Ship to The Cross Hands on the left were all fields behind a stone wall covered in ivy, until you came to the quarry, which was the local rubbish tip. Past 'Orchard House' was 'The Corderies', where Grammar School teacher Bath Stafford Morse and his family lived. Mr Morse and his wife had a big influence on the development of Alveston in the 50's and 60's. Mr Morse always kept his dustbin on the low stone wall at the front of the house, so one of our favourite tricks was to get a cracker or jumping jack as they were called and light it and drop it in the bin, put the lid on and run. Next morning Mr Morse would ring Mr Bosworth at the school to try to identify the culprits, which of course he never did.

At the back of this house were two little stone cottages. In one lived an old man called Driver Williams and his lodger Mrs Tuffin and family, and in the other side lived Ernie Mills and wife. Next down was a small paddock in which stood an old gypsy caravan on high wheels and beautifully painted. A succession of people lived in this caravan until they found a house, including my own brother Ted, Dick Coleman, Mrs Shergold and children, Ken Bradley, to name but a few.

Further down was the house and shop of Mr Hedley Williams who was a carpenter and wheelwright. Just inside his gate was a glass cabinet in which he advertised his wares. I can't remember how many times we smashed that glass with catapults. Next door was Alveston Post Office run by Mr and Mrs Bert Burgess. Mr Burgess was an officer of some sort in the Home Guard, whilst Mrs Burgess was another tireless worker with the local women's groups.

In one of the two houses next door lived local postman Sid Wilton and family. Now Sid would tell you who your letter was from before you opened it, and if for some reason he didn't know, the next day he would ask you. In the other one lived an old Scottish couple called Mr and Mrs Bandy Burns, which is why it is named 'Ballochmyle'. Later on my sister and her husband Ken Murdoch lived here. Next door was the local builder whom I worked for when I left school, Mr Frank 'Tooker' Curtis and family.

Now Tooker was a man possessed of a great sense of humour. He was involved in a lot of things in the village without actually doing anything. As far as he was concerned, tomorrow would do, and he was a bit like that with his work. When we had to work at places like Pilning or Charfield he would say to me "Bring your flask and sandwiches tomorrow Cuthbert (this was his favourite name for me, because he knew that I hated it) because we won't be home for lunch".

The next morning out he would come with a bag containing two flasks of coffee and a mountain of sandwiches. We would trundle off to work in his old Morris 8, about 12.30 he would look at his watch and say "My gosh, is that the time? You carry on here Cuthbert, I promised to meet a rep in The Ship at 1 o'clock I must fly", and off he went. He would return at about 4pm to pick me up smelling very strongly of brandy, and off we would go home with his mass of sandwiches still intact. I don't know what Mrs Curtis thought of that but knowing Frank I expect he had a very plausible excuse. I remember that not long before Frank died, he was leaning on his front gate, when a woman who was passing, stopped to ask him how he was feeling. "Oh, I don't know" said Frank, "one foot in the grave and one foot on a bar of soap, I think!"

Past Tooker's place was a row of cottages, I think the Stevens family lived in one and where the shop now is, lived Bert Weekes, brother of Nailer Weekes (of Miss Osbourne fame), also Bernie Burcome and family.

Now we come to Quarry Road. I won't name all the people who live there but I would like to mention one, Mr Robert Vizard. Together with my father and uncle Tom they were the local poachers and Mr Fixits. During the war when things were scarce we and many others lived on rabbits supplied by these three men. I shall never forget the days and sometimes nights that we went with them and Bob's ferret Moscow Joe, which he carried in his inside pocket, on a rabbit catching mission. Sometimes we would catch up to thirty rabbits in one go. They also took us long netting at night but we had to keep quiet and take no part in the actual setting up of the net, but I still remember how to do it, and the things they taught us I put to good use later on in my life.

Bob once told me how he had been poaching on his own one day - he had netted the warren or bury as we called it, and just put the ferret in the hole when the gamekeeper appeared, Bob quickly picked up as many nets as he could but was forced to take flight and leave Joe in the bury. The gamekeeper shouted at him to stop and then let fly with both barrels and as Bob put it "He made the dust fly out of me overcoat". He made his escape at the expense of losing his nets but he said that he went back later and recovered Joe who came to his call.

Robert was also the life and soul of The Cross Hands hotel and would keep us entranced with his tales of when he served in the Great War. One of these tales was of the time he was in the trenches in France, the Officer blew his whistle and over the top they went. Bob suddenly realised they were outnumbered ten to one, so he turned on his heels and went to run back when something got hung up in his legs. When he looked down he saw that it was a hare, so according to him he gave it a kick and said "Get out of the bloody way and let somebody run who can". Someone said later that he never actually went abroad. He was also a singer of some note, and he used to render a song called 'Nightingales in the Branches', when he'd had a few pints with great gusto. He was a proper character.

Right at the top of Quarry Road where 'Costers Close' now stands, was a little cottage in which lived Charlie Coster and family. Charlie worked as a farm labourer for Mr Tom Harraway at Marlwood farm where the golf club now stands. Charlie gave great service to Alveston Down football club over the years, both as a player and as a manager. At times, he ran the club almost on his own and I can remember him playing when we were short when he was well into his fifties.

Further across in the fields were two stone cottages, in one lived my uncle Bob 'Sparrow' Curtis and family, in the other lived Sid Vizard and family. I remember that they had a black mongrel dog called Bonzo, and every time the air raid siren sounded Bonzo would jump on the wall, put his nose in the air and howl in unison with it. Sometimes he heard it when we hadn't.

Back down Quarry Road on the opposite side of the road was a stone stile which led down some concrete steps, through a wicket gate and along a footpath and across two fields, then you came to Savery's Corner where the shops are now. These steps also led to a limestone quarry complete with lime kiln which was used as a rubbish tip for years until it was filled in and it is now the local playing field. As kids this was another of our haunts much to the disgust of our mothers because we got so dirty. We spent many summer holidays there chasing and killing rats and throwing stones at the hoards of bats that came out at dusk.

In this quarry was a house called '21 Steps', in which lived an old man called Fifield and his family. The house was below the level of the road. At night we would get a wet sack and manoeuvre it onto the chimney with a long stick then wait for results, when the occupants came out coughing, spluttering and cursing. This house was demolished and buried when they filled the quarry in.

On the other side of the road across the field where 'Quarry Mead' now stands, was a farm owned by Mr Joe Paynes and family, whilst on the left was a low stone wall with a drop of some thirty to forty feet into the old quarry, I remember that someone came out of the pub one dark night and wanting to obey a call of nature leapt over this wall and landed forty feet below in the quarry, breaking his leg in the process.

Thus we arrive back at The Cross Hands pub, having completed the circle.

Herbie Curtis

Why don't we step inside for a pint and a chat.

The Cross Hands of Alveston

Talk (Local Dialect)

On the subject of chatting, you'll already have noticed my attempts to portray the way people speak. The local dialect is very much 'West Country' and used to be far stronger when I was a lad, probably because we didn't spent our days glued to the television!

This is a typical conversation between two boys of that time spoken in the local dialect. One boy is cycling up the road when he meets his friend and the conversation went like this

Tom: "Mornin Herb, wer bis thee off to then?"

Herb: "Ello Tom, well! we bin a run out of coal an I be off down Thornbury to get a hunnerd weight on me bike."

Tom: "Thee ousent push a hunnerd weight up that hill on thee own."

Herb: "I oull, I've done it before."

Tom: " Thee ousent, then, I better come and give 'e a hand."

Herb: "No, thass alright."

Tom: "Well I bent doin nothin else."

Herb: "Oh awright then. Yer, why bissn't thee at school today anyroad."

Tom: "Well, I wunt very well last night so our mam said I better have today off an see ow I felt tomorrow."

Herb: "Thees look alright to I."

Tom: "Course I be, you twerp, I just wanted a day off school thass all."

Herb: "Oh well come on then, cos I gotta get back and light the fire fore are ol' man do get home, or else I'll get a good hiding."

Ferreting

Let me now take you on one of our rabbit catching trips. My father would usually say to us the night before "You'd better be up early in the morning if you want to come with us."

The next morning I would be up bright and early. After lighting the fire I would go out and start loading the nets into a sack. Our spaniel dog, Trixie, would be leaping about in anticipation. I would tie her up, pat her on the head and say "You're not coming today old girl, I'm afraid." At which she would lie down and watch me with her big brown eyes, sulking.

The spade and billhook would be tied on the crossbar of the bicycle, whilst the ferret box was strapped on the carrier. After breakfast came the part I didn't like, which was getting the ferrets out of their cage and transferring them to the carrying box. They would come out of their warm straw, half asleep, with their little red eyes blinking in the light. If you didn't handle them firmly you were asking for a nasty bite on the fingers. When everything was ready, the shotgun broken down into sections, and concealed in father's old ARP overcoat, off we would go to meet my uncle, at a previously arranged meeting place. When he arrived we'd set off.

The morning was usually cold, with frost or snow lingering under the hedges on the side of the road. At that time of day all we were liable to see was the local postman cycling along on his rounds or the milk lorry collecting churns from the farms. We took note of the pheasants scratching about under the oak trees, looking for acorns. That was for future reference, when we only had the gun. After a while we would arrive at our destination, hide our bicycles behind the hedge and shoulder our gear.

Off we would go, through the crisp grass to the first warren, or bury, as they are called in Glo'shire. Whilst the men were cutting back the brambles in the hedge, and putting nets over the holes, we boys would be going up and down the field looking for boltholes (or popholes as we called them), which might be hidden in the grass some way from the main bury.

Eventually every hole was netted and the ferret was taken from the box and dropped into one of the holes. Once again you had to be very careful because they didn't like the cold ground on their feet and would sometimes whip round and bite your hand. After the ferret had gone in everyone was still and silent watching the nets. Sometimes the ferret came straight back out of another hole and had to be picked up and put back in again. After a bit someone would hold their finger up for silence and suddenly whoosh! Out would shoot a rabbit into one of the nets, to be grabbed up by whoever was nearest and quickly despatched with a chop behind the ears with the heel of the hand. Then the net would be replaced. Sometimes you would hear a swishing noise and a rabbit would go away down the hedge, having come out of a hidden hole, followed by curses and shouts of "Who forgot to net that bloody hole?!".

We might have half a dozen rabbits out of that bury before they decided there were no more in there. The ferret and nets were retrieved and on we would go to the next one with the same procedure. We didn't have everything our own way however, sometimes the ferret would refuse to come out, it had either killed a rabbit in the bury or it had curled up and gone to sleep. Either way it meant that we had to use a liner ferret to find out where it was. This was usually a polecat ferret with a collar on to which was attached a length of string. It usually went straight to the other ferret and you knew roughly by the length of line where it was. After putting your ear to the ground and listening to the bumps and noises you pinpointed where you thought they were. Then came the job of digging down to them. Sometimes you might dig a few holes until you finally located them and dragged them out, usually with the rabbit as well.

On a bad day this might take a couple of hours, which put us all behind, but normally all went smoothly.

In time we might have two dozen rabbits in the sack. The men usually liked to get back to the pub for their cider by one o'clock. They would put a couple of rabbits in their pocket to sell in the pub, the rest of the gear we had to take home. The nets were hung in the shed to dry, the gun was put back in the cupboard under the stairs, the ferrets were put back in their cage and fed with bread and milk. Then we were free to go and get our own dinner. The rabbits were usually gutted in the field and the insides left for the foxes. When we got home they were taken out of the sacks and hung up on hooks in the back kitchen. After that we were glad to curl up on the sofa, by the open fire, and go to sleep, I can tell 'ee.

Romance

No good book is complete without a bit of romance and mine is no exception. Now the majority of boys of my age had no interest in the opposite sex. All we ever wanted to do was play football or cricket, so unless girls could do either of these, we completely ignored them.

I suppose I was fourteen or fifteen years old at the time in mention, we were playing cricket in the Jubilee Hall field as usual, when suddenly this girl appeared over the style at the top of the field. As soon as I saw her my heart did a quick somersault. It appeared that her name was Yvonne and she came from Thornton Heath in Surrey, which of course as far as I knew could have been in Timbuctoo. She was on school holiday and was staying with her aunt, Addie Riddiford who lived at the top of the Hall field.

She must have been smitten the same as me because we became inseparable. I lost interest in cricket and football. We used to go on long walks together, down Greenhill lane and on the old golf links. I would tell her all about the wild flowers, trees, animals, and birds and she was very interested in country life, because I suppose she lived in a suburb of London. I had a lot of competition from other local boys but as soon as Yvonne came down on holiday she made a bee line for me and I would be waiting.

Herbie Curtis as a young man

This went on for a couple of years and aunt Addie became aware of the situation, she didn't approve of me. She tried to keep Yvonne in by locking her in the bedroom, but she would jump down on to the shed and escape to see me. I hated aunt Addie! We carried on like this until I was about seventeen. I used to hold her hand whilst we were walking but that was as far as it went.

One lovely summer day we were walking on the golf links. I had just carved a heart with the initials "H. C. & Y. R." on one of the beech trees (which is still there, 'cos I went and had a look). Anyway, it came on to rain heavily, a thunder storm, and as I only had on a shirt and trousers and Yvonne a thin summer dress, we took shelter under an ivy covered lime kiln which, again, is still there. We huddled up closely together and I put my arms round her to keep her warm, but all of a sudden we both began to tremble violently and she began to cry. We didn't know what was happening to us. It wasn't until a long time after that I understood that this was the first stirring of young love. I don't know how long we stayed there, but suddenly it stopped raining and we resumed our walk. I took her home and we loitered on the stile for a bit, then she threw her arms around me and gave me a passionate kiss. Then she was gone.

I carried on exchanging letters with her for sometime after that, but I never saw her again. Eventually I went to do my National Service and I lost touch with her and the rest is history. However! that is not the end of the story because recently I bumped into her cousin, Bob Riddiford and told him about this. He is still in touch with Yvonne and tells me that she still remembers this vividly, and sends me all her love. I hope this tale doesn't embarrass the young lady involved. I myself think that it's a great credit to the way we were brought up, that we managed to overcome temptation. Ah! The joy and pain of young love.

Finish yer pint and we'll leave the Cross Hands now and take a walk around some of the outlying areas.

OUTLYING AREAS

Just up the road is Olddown, where the book began. Let's head back into Alveston from that direction.

On the left before you get to the Strode set back up a drive, was a little cottage in which lived Dr Rhind and family. I don't know what he was a doctor of but he looked a very smart gentleman indeed, as he walked up the road with his trilby hat, smart suit with brown spats and ivory headed cane. He used to catch the bus into Bristol every morning. His son Colin was the local Boy Scout leader.

Turning back down Vattingstone Lane, there were fields on both sides until you came to a red brick house on the right in which lived Eddie and Audrey Atherton. During the war these fields were covered in piles of rocks, so say to prevent enemy gliders from landing. These fields are now the site of Marlwood School and playing fields. During the early part of the war they were used by pilots and learner pilots from Filton Airfield, to practice landings. It was also our cricket pitch and we didn't think much of them using it, so we used to deliberately run in front of them when they were landing to put them off.

Gipsies at Vattingstone Lane

Further down on the left was a little piece of ground known to us as gypsy patch, there were usually gipsies in residence there. On to the top of Elberton Hill then down the hill and turn right into Sweet Watering, the hedges along this road were always alive with birds and rabbits and the woods were a haven for jays and magpies, pheasants and the occasional kestrel. On along this winding road until you came to a farm on the right which was the HQ and depot of H. A .King & Sons, transport contractors.

Further on up was a lodge owned by Kington House, I can't remember who lived there. Then you come to the dreaded Mumbly's Hill. According to my friend Rodney Webb this hill got its name from the fact that on a Saturday some of the village men would venture down the hill and would not reappear until Sunday night. When they came back they were shaking and trembling and couldn't stand properly and mumbled incoherent stories about having seen giant snakes, pink elephants, fiery dragons and other terrible sights, hence the name Mumbly's. He was of the opinion that the Oldbury cider might have had something to do with it.

Turning right back towards Alveston, there were two small cottages, in the first lived Jack 'Shonto' Vizard and family, in the other lived Tom Iles and his wife. Tom used to sport a big white beard and rode an old fashioned upright bicycle, while his wife was a wizened, bent over old woman who wore a black shawl over her head and muttered to herself incessantly, again I wasn't quite sure if she wasn't a witch. Tom had a hen which he called Rachel, which roosted on the handlebars of his bicycle and would sing with him. He was always asking me to come and listen to Rachel singing.

Then on up the lane to a farm on the right in which lived farmer Batten and family, afterwards the home of the Jenner family. And so back to Vattingstone Lane.

At the bottom of Alveston Hill was Marlwood Grange and its lodges, set back in the woods and owned at that time by Captain Jenkins. Then on around to Vilner, the Abbey and Little Abbey Farm, owned by the Watkins family. Then down Shellards lane to a cottage on the left, where Jekka Herbs now is, lived Mr and Mrs Selwood, who at that time was the local post woman.

On the right was a farm owned by the Joneses. Across the fields on the left were Owls Nest Farm and Dodsmoor, where lived Owen Radford and the Shepherds respectively. Then head down the hill to the little hamlet of Itchington, now bisected by the motorway. Turn right to Earthcott, which hasn't altered for five hundred years - a little hamlet with a few farms and cottages, and its own little school. Then turn right up the Iron Acton Road to the old church and Rudgeway.

Now I shall return to St. Helens church and resume my journey along to The Masons Arms public house which was where we considered Alveston ended. Opposite the church were a pair of semi detached cottages. In one side lived a council worker called Mr Gazzard and I think in the other lived nurse Baker. Next to that was Mr and Mrs Ball and their son Ted.

Amongst those living in this row of red brick houses was our Headmaster, Mr Reg Bosworth. I remember him telling us during history lessons that the only two dates he could remember were, the Battle of Hastings and the Battle of Bosworth Field. Beyond lived our local policeman, PC Keane. Further down was our infant teacher Mrs Tomkins and others I can't remember.

On the other side of the road was the old vicarage, at that time occupied by Mr F. W. Walmsley, our beloved vicar. I remember that one Saturday the local football team, Alveston Down Sports, of which I was a proud member, had stopped to pick up a couple of the team opposite the church. At that time we used to have an old coach which we called the 'Silver Bullet'. Mr Walmsley came from the vicarage drive and asked whom we were playing. Someone shouted "Arsehole". Quick as a flash the vicar replied "Oh well done, I hope you give them a jolly good licking" and carried on his way.

Another thing I remember him for is this, every Thursday afternoon he was in the habit of going to Miss Osbornes in the Street, there they would have tea and cakes and a good old chat. One day when I was working there they had finished tea and the vicar said "That cake was so nice Miss Osborne, that I wouldn't say no if you asked me to have some more". Well what could the poor woman do!

On past the vicarage and set back in was a big house called 'The Glebe', this was owned by the Burrbidge family. Very often we were invited into the lounge for coffee and biscuits while Mrs Burrbidge's sister entertained us by playing a piece of music called 'Galloping Horses' on the piano. I think that was the only tune she knew.

On the same side was a modern house called 'Heatherfield', in which lived the McMahons. Next door to that was two small cottages, in which lived Charlie Biddle's father and an old lady called Mrs Giles. Next was the blacksmith shop and forge belonging to Mr Charlie Smith and family. Mr Smith was a fervent churchgoer and his son Arthur sang in the church choir. This blacksmith's shop was working into the 50's. Once again it has been converted into a private house.

In the houses opposite lived Mrs Maggie Hadrell and Frank Spouse and family. Frank was a Geordie, and at one time ran the local youth club. His accent was so thick that we had a terrible time trying to understand what he was trying to say to us. I can't remember the others who lived there.

Just past these was Mr Billy Champion's builders yard. Down over the bank lived Mr and Mrs Kemp and boys Brian and Dave. In the little cottage on the side of this there lived Archie Payne and family, known to us as Agony, the son of Joe Payne of Alveston.

Back over the road again, next to Charlie Smith's, there lived a family called Outerside. They had a son who we called Storming Norman, who was an absolute maniac on a motorbike. Then we came to Dolly Balls corner. This was named after an old lady who had a shop in her front room which sold sweets, cigarettes and papers. During the fifties this was demolished along with a couple of others including 'Sniper' Art Moss's house, Nurse Baker's and another one, to make room for road widening. This only left the cottage owned by the Ellis family, which is still there.

In the cottage past here, called 'The Mount', lived the Whiteman family. Then next door was an old lady called, I think, Jackson. On the opposite side of this was the Black and White Cafe and filling station. Behind this was the British Legion Hut, scene of many a whist drive and dance during the war.

And now we reach The Masons Arms, run by Mr Jim Wilson, ex Leeds and Bristol City goalkeeper. I think I will leave Rudgeway for some other historian to describe.

Turning right at The Masons Arms and down the hill we come to Lower Hazel, which was considered to be a part of Alveston. In a cottage on the right at the top, lived the Saxtons. Then on down the hill to Valley Farm which was owned by Fred Moxham and later by 'Bubbles' Ford, his wife and son, Richard, who sadly died very young. Next door lived an old lady called Mrs Felthham.

On the opposite side of the lane, across from the big cedar trees, was a large country house, in which lived the Baldings, who owned a coal company in Bristol. We used to call this house the 'monkey house' because it was rumoured that they kept zoo animals there. This was later owned by General Sir Charles Alfrey and family.

At Lower Hazel Farm lived Mr and Mrs Jimmy Olive. Jimmy was an old time farmer and did all his farm work with horses, as far as I remember they never owned a tractor. They were devout chapel goers and they practised what they preached. As children, we used to help them with the hay making, for which we were rewarded with a big hunk of fresh bread smothered with farmhouse butter and a huge piece of cheese, plus one penny each. We were quite happy with this because we were always hungry and it was gratefully received.

Alas! We were not always so helpful to the poor old man, as we used to steal his apples and eggs all the time. He never offered us any violence, although we certainly deserved it. I can remember once, when we were raiding his orchard, he stood there and said "I dwunt mind 'ee aven the fruit bways, but dwun 'ee break the boughs about." Another time he caught us chopping a tree about. He gave us a sermon about good and evil, then gave us a penny each and made us promise to go to chapel on the next Sunday. We didn't go of course.

He had a farm labourer called Jack Davis, who was as old as he was. But he was a completely different kettle of fish. He used to give us a good clout with his belt buckle, if he caught us, which wasn't often. One time, we were helping him to load mangolds (beets) on his tipping cart pulled by his old horse Bob. Someone removed the securing pin which prevented the cart from tipping. Jack shouted "Gee up Bob!" and of course as the horse jerked forward, up went the cart and all the mangolds went rolling down the hill. We scarpered with Jack shouting after us "Come back yer you little buggers. Cassn't 'ee yer, I a' whoopin on 'ee!" We used to mimic him when he was ploughing.

"Forrat" he would say, or "Cum 'ee up Prince," or "Cum over 'ull 'ee Captain!" Then we would pelt him with lumps of clay, until he chased us off. But mostly, we were on very good terms with them and we did help them a lot.

Further on, under the golf links was a big house in which lived the Baileys. At the side of this house surrounded by high walls was a Quaker's burial ground, in which stood a giant Wellingtonia tree, which we called the 'punch tree', because you could hit it hard and not hurt your hand at all. We didn't hang about there much, because with the laurels and the gravestones, it was dark and ghostly and scared us.

At the bottom on the left, there was a long cottage in which lived people called Crystal. On up the hill on the left, was the small holding and market garden of Len Walker and his sister Lena. They worked very hard digging this up with a spade, tending and weeding it. Len would take the produce to Bristol in a pony and trap to sell it.

Returning back down the hill you came to Greenhill Lane, which took you back to Alveston via a stony bridle path. We used to catch fireflies here on balmy summer evenings, and put them in a jam jar where they would flash their little blue and green lights, like little diamonds. The golf links, Hartygrove and Lower Wolfridge were also the haunt of nightingales, which sang all night. We once counted seven different birds singing at the same time. We also found their nests, but we never touched them because it was considered unlucky.

I recently paid a visit to the vicinity. I didn't hear any nightingales, so I presume that like a lot of my childhood friends, they're gone. But I hope because of this book, they're not forgotten.

Herbie Curtis

SCHOOL DAYS IN WARTIME

I would like now to describe my school days, or at least what I can remember of them. My first memories are of walking to Rudgeway school along the A38. I remember we used to thumb lifts on army lorries, and once we got a lift in a Bren gun carrier. In the summer, we used to play marbles in the gutter on the way home. Some chance of doing that nowadays.

First thing in the morning we had assembly, followed by a hymn and a prayer. Sometimes the local vicar, Mr Walmsley would join us for this. Then we all went to our respective classrooms, where we had the register or roll call. Then we got down to our lessons.

At playtime, the boys and girls normally played in their respective yards, but during P.E. lessons we were mixed. The girls played games like skipping, bouncing the ball against the wall, tag, hopscotch, as well as various group games like creep mouse, oranges and lemons, piggy in the middle, and of course daddies and mummies. The boys would play Cowboys and Indians, conkers, tag, cricket, fighting, and most popular of all, football. We used to play inter-school football matches with Olveston school, which was a truly local derby because we all knew each other.

During all these playtime activities the headmaster, Mr Bosworth (to whom this book is dedicated), would watch over us, although half the time we didn't know this. If anybody got out of hand they were quickly dealt with by a couple of cuts on the hand with his cane, in front of the whole class. I was the recipient of this on many occasions, and I can tell you that I was never in a hurry to invite a repeat performance.

If we repeatedly played truant, we could expect a visit from Mr Cooper, the school inspector. He would come to your house to see your parents, and again a good hiding would quickly follow. The same thing applied to the law. If you did something wrong, the local policeman, Mr Keane, went and saw your parents. It was up to them to punish you. Of course if Mr Keane caught you red-handed, he would give you a lecture and a clip round the ear himself, before marching you home for your parents to give you another! I never knew him take any local children to court, and we respected him utterly.

During the summer term they would hold the school sports, the prizes for winning were sixpenny savings stamps. We used to train for weeks before to win this great sum. For instance my cousin and I would tie our legs together with a school tie and would run to school and back home again at night. We became so good that nobody could touch us. We trained hard for every race, consequently one or other of us would win every race, and we would go home rich.

We also used to attend Sunday School most Sundays. The main reason being that if you attended so many times you qualified for the annual visit to Weston-Super-Mare but, having said that, despite ourselves it did instil Christian beliefs and morals in us, which I think is sadly lacking today. For instance, respect for our elders, compassion for the sick, handicapped and less able and to help one another where ever you could.

We knew everybody in the village and they knew us, we could go to almost any house in the village and be welcomed with warmth and friendship despite our cheekiness because we were one of them, we were family and we did our best not to betray this trust. No-one had to lock their door in Alveston at that time.

During the war years we thought up and painted posters for Spitfire week and battleship week and dig for victory etc. We were issued with green cards entitling us to so many weeks off school to help with the potato harvest.

We worked a lot with Italian prisoners of war, which meant we learned to speak very passable Italian, especially the swear words. I can't remember them now of course but I never forgot when I got into trouble to hold my arms outstretched, roll my eyes up and say "No Comprendi". There was one character who we used to call Merrygrow, but a think his name was probably Amerigo, who knew all the tricks of the trade and taught most of them to us.

I can't remember when we were issued with gas masks but I know that you never went anywhere without them slung round your neck, and every so often you received tuition on how to put them on. I also remember that after air raids on Bristol, we would pick up incendiary bombs on the way to school, some spent and occasionally live ones. These latter didn't worry us but caused a big commotion at school where they were hurriedly placed in a bucket of sand and the bomb disposal team called.

I can remember coming out of school one afternoon and seeing an aeroplane plunging to the ground at Silverhill Brake. I was the first person on the scene; in fact the tail wheel was still spinning when I arrived. The plane was on fire and the pilot was still in the cockpit, but I knew he was dead by the state of the wreckage. Some men appeared and chased me away. I took a long time to get over that. I can remember quite a few plane crashes in the locality including one at Mumbleys, a spitfire I think. The pilot, PO Locke is buried near the war memorial at St Helens church. I can vaguely remember the street parties on VE day but everything seems to be a blur afterwards.

School holidays were one round of pleasure as far as we were concerned and never came too soon, especially the six week summer holiday. We would leave home early in the morning and often our parents wouldn't see us again until it was dark. We found our own food, living on hen's eggs which we stole around farmer's haymows or barns, or during the spring on moorhens eggs, or pheasant eggs which we boiled up in an old tin. This was supplemented by swedes or turnips which we ate raw, and by apples, blackberries nuts and other fruit. Our parents weren't worried at all by this behaviour and we felt completely safe, which is more than can be said for nowadays.

Adjacent to the Square was a great big dark wood called "Wolfridge". It was a mature wood of big oak trees, beeches, ash and a few pine trees, with laurels, ferns and brambles growing below. We spent hours in the depth of this wood playing cowboys and Indians and war games. We constructed tree houses in the top most branches of the bigger trees, thirty or forty feet off the ground, and so well camouflaged that no one could find them. We used to borrow camouflage netting off the soldiers at the Jubilee Hall ground and haul up to the top of these trees. We constructed long bows with sharpened points to the arrows which were accurate up to fifty and sixty yards, as many a local cat or dog would have testified.

When we weren't shooting at old tins we used to hunt rabbits, crows or magpies or other creatures with these, sometimes we used catapults. Later on we had air guns but we had trouble getting the pellets for these and they were always getting confiscated by our parents, so we fell back on bows and arrows. We got to learn all the habits of the country birds and animals, and could imitate most of them perfectly, for instance, I have known us imitate the sound of a rabbit caught in a snare and entice a fox into range of our bows, or we would imitate wood pigeons with the same intentions.

No bird's nest was safe from us as we knew exactly where to find them. For instance, the fields at that time especially around Greenhill abounded with skylarks in the spring, the skies were full of their lovely song. We would hide in the grass and wait for them to slowly descend, give them a couple of minutes to get on their nest, then jump up and run to the spot where they went down. Now they always ran a few yards from their nest before flying, so we used to stick a cricket stump or a piece of wood in the ground. To this we attached a piece of string, then we went carefully round and round in ever widening circles and it wasn't long before we found the nest. The eggs were so well camouflaged with their brown and purple squiggles, that we had to be careful not to stand on them. We also used this method with peewits and partridges.

There were also butterflies in great numbers, red admirals, marbled whites, orange tips, brimstones, painted ladies and on Greenhill and the Golf links there were hundreds of little blue ones. Also on Greenhill we used to find the rare bee orchid.

The old golf links were a favourite haunt of ours, the gorse bushes abounded with linnets, yellow hammers, goldfinches, bullfinches, and hundreds of rabbits. The air was full of bird song, while the sound of the church bells in the distance seemed to make time stand still - it did for us anyway. We just didn't worry about time, we had all our lives in front of us.

Incidentally, the golf links were also the haunt of sweethearts in the summertime and there used to be a big stone called the kissing stone on which young lovers could sit and cuddle. It isn't there now because we got some levers and put under it and rolled it down the hill into the gorse bushes. Of course, another of our tricks was spying on them and generally making ourselves a nuisance.

Our sworn enemies were the Rudgeway gang, who shall remain anonymous. They would attack and burn down our camps and we would retaliate in similar fashion. Woe betide you if they caught you on your own, you were violently roughed up amongst other atrocities. We did the same to them of course, but it was all relatively harmless.

One of our ploys was to stretch a piano type wire across a steep path in Wolfridge, about knee high, then we would send out a decoy who was good at running, to locate them and let himself be pursued, he would lead them back while the rest of us lay in ambush. After the decoy had gone by we tightened the wire and brought them all tumbling down, a battle royal then ensued until someone got really hurt, then we would all scatter and disappear. Or we would get them coming up the hill, we had a big lorry tyre at the top which was stuffed with paper and straw and soaked in paraffin, we would light this and send it hurling down at them. Sometimes we would set fire to bicycle tyres and whirl them around our heads so that pieces of burning rubber flew off in all directions, much to the consternation of our own infantry. See - we invented napalm long before the Yanks! Of course we got a lot of these ideas from the Wizard or the Hotspur or some other comic which we used to swap with each other.

We used to wander far and wide and the days never seemed long enough for us. We were very happy during the war when they brought in Double British Summertime, which meant it was light until twelve at night. In the winter we would make toboggans and spend the snowy days either on the old golf links at Oldown or else on Marlwood where it was steeper.

At Christmas time we would go from door to door carol singing and we made quite a bit of money at this. Then on New Year's morning we were out early with our faces and hair blackened with charcoal, 'firstfooting'. I remember the rhyme well, it went "Old year out, new year in, glass of cider, glass of gin, open the door and let luck in.". You were then let into the house and had to walk around the table, then they gave you a penny and sometimes an apple or a mince pie, then you walked out of the door on to the next house. The money we made at this went towards buying us new shoes or clothes. We used to wear hand me down clothes or clothes that kind neighbours gave us, after their own children had grown out of them.

Of course in between there were parties given by the WRVS and the Sunday school and others which were well attended by us. Although we were always hungry we were a healthy lot and never really got ill, except for the usual things like measles, mumps, chicken pox and common colds. During the war we used to have vitamins given to us in the form of cod-liver oil, rosehip syrup, malted milk, glucose and blackcurrant drinks. Christmas during the war years was a fairly low key event because you just couldn't get anything like bananas and oranges even if you could afford them.

We were fortunate that my father kept pigs so we would have pork or sometimes chicken for our dinner. Turkey was a rare commodity for anyone. Vegetables were no problem as we all had gardens or allotments. My father was Secretary of the 'Small Pig Keepers Association'. Members were allocated a certain amount of pig meal, as that too was rationed. To supplement this we would be given a sack and sent around all the oak trees in the vicinity gathering acorns, which the pigs loved. We daren't go home until we had a sack full, but it was all worth it on the day the pig was killed.

Early in the morning Mr Kendall, the butcher, would appear. The poor pig would be squealing its head off. There was then a big commotion with everyone running with buckets of hot water to scald the carcass and scrape the hair off. The pig was cut up, jointed and soaked in salt water to preserve it. The sides were hung up in the kitchen, to be salted every so often whilst the head was used to make brawn. Even the insides and trotters were used to make chitterlings or faggots. What we kids wanted most was the bladder, which we used to blow up with a straw and used to play football. Mr Kendall once told me that the only part of a pig that you couldn't eat was the squeal. After the butcher had signed the licence and been paid everything returned to normal.

Toys were usually home-made wooden affairs, like forts or Tommy guns with ratchets which made realistic noises. For the girls there were dolls houses or rag dolls or wooden train sets or skipping ropes. We used to make our own decorations with coloured paper chains and bells and we always managed to get some holly and a Christmas tree from somewhere. I can still remember the anticipation of eating the

Christmas pudding very carefully in case you swallowed the silver thrupenny piece that was supposed to be in there but seldom was.

My father also used to make roly poly puddings which consisted of flour, currants, pieces of candy, suet and sultanas which he rolled into a cloth and put in the wash boiler, these lasted for days and you always knew when he had been cooking because the cloths hung on the line like tattered flags.

The original grate and oven in the living room

Another staple food of ours was rabbit stew with swede and onions. There was always a stew pot boiling away on the hearth and a rice pudding in the oven, when it wasn't full of damp socks or gloves.

Come to think of it things haven't changed much because the same grate is still there today and they still cook on it as always.

I think that I should also mention the American soldiers, the Yanks as we called them. They were based at Tortworth just up the road and used the A38 quite a lot. They also used to bring their rubbish, or garbage, to the tip at Alveston on a daily basis. This was a veritable goldmine to us kids, they were so wasteful they would throw away unopened tins of coffee, malted milk, bouillon powder and dextrose tablets, which were luxuries to us and well appreciated by our parents.

They also threw away packets of cigarettes and tins of tobacco, we were all chain smokers by the time we were thirteen. I could well remember those names now, Camel, Old Gold, Philip Morris, Chesterfield and Lucky Strike. I can remember once we found a box of contraceptives. We of course didn't know what they were, we thought they were balloons so we blew them up, tied them on strings and paraded up and down the road, much to the amusement of the local men, but the embarrassment of the local ladies who thought we were hooligans.

We used to give the drivers of the lorries the names of local girls in exchange for gum or chocolate. Unlike a lot of local husbands, we were very sorry to see them go. After the war we returned to the usual life of playing football and delivering papers and eventually being called up to do National Service.

On reflection in my old age, I think I lived just at the right time, when I hear of the terrible things which are happening in the village now a days, things that were unheard of and unthinkable in my day. I despair for the future generations and I certainly wouldn't want to be born and grow up in this modern age. I thoroughly enjoyed and was very content with my childhood and I will be quite happy to spend the rest of my life with the memories of Wolfridge wood and my childhood haunts and friends.

Epilogue

People do say to I, "Woss wanna write thic rubbish vor?".

I do thenk to meself: Well! When I do be dyud an gone, everything us I do know is gone as well, and t'ould be a pity to lose all that 'ouldn't it, you?

S'no wat I myun?

Herbie Curtis

Biography

Herbert Curtis, known to one and all as Herbie, was born in the early 1930's. He spent his formative years in and around the village of Alveston in South Gloucestershire, England. He spent time in the army and turned his hand to many trades, particularly the craft of Stone Masonry. In the mid 1990s he was finally persuaded to turn his hand to writing.

Herbie died in 1998, but has left behind a legacy set both in stone and memories.

About the Book

My father loved telling a good story. He was a natural raconteur and the life and soul of any gathering. I spent my childhood listening to him tell tales of his youth and time in the army.

As he mentions in the forward, I spent years nagging him to record some of these tales, making notes for myself so I could get more detail on the more memorable events.

I finally got him to start recording some of his memories onto cassette. Once he got into the swing of things, his enthusiasm for the idea picked up and he started writing an actual memoir.

His first draft was printed as a small pamphlet for a charity fund-raiser. He received so much encouragement and additional material that he started on a much expanded version.

When he died in 1998, the work was mostly complete, but some sections were still on cassette and some were just in note form.

In the few days after he died, my fiancée and I worked on the incomplete manuscript. We spent many hours at my dining room table. I would read the handwritten text aloud and she would type it up.

The result was a hastily edited and photocopied booklet that we were able to make available to give to family and friends.

In the following year I went through the cassette recordings to add extra details and turned some of the sections that existed only as notes into the stories I remembered dad telling me as a kid.

We added some old family photographs to supplement the text. The complete book was printed in 1999, once again as a photocopied booklet that raised funds for charity.

On the 25th Anniversary of this printing, I am proud to finally publish dad's memoir as an actual book.

Anyone who read the original booklet will find only a few additions that have come to light over the years, but the text remains as timeless and engaging as it ever was.

Ryan Curtis

Milton Keynes UK
Ingram Content Group UK Ltd.
UKHW052245280524
443311UK00008B/158

9 780645 780826